PERPETUAL
WATERFALLS

DAVID ASHBEE

PERPETUAL WATERFALLS

David Ashbee.

ENITHARMON PRESS 1989

First published in 1989
by the Enitharmon Press
40 Rushes Road
Petersfield
Hampshire GU32 3BW

Cover design by Julian Bell

ISBN 0 905289 84 6

The Enitharmon Press acknowledges financial
assistance from Southern Arts

Set in Monotype Ehrhardt by
Boase Press, Monmouth, Gwent

Printed in Great Britain by
Antony Rowe Ltd, Chippenham, Wiltshire

CONTENTS

For the Prema Poets and all who have tutored us,
without whom many of the poems in this collection might
never have sniffed the air.

Thanks are due to the following for the original
publication or broadcasting of a number of poems:
BBC Radio 4 and Blandford Press (for 'After the
Woodpecker'); BBC2 TV and judges of the 1978 *Sunday*
Times competition (for 'The Archaeologist'); *South*
West Review (for 'Hoover' and 'Chessboard Weather');
Westwords (for 'Caretaker' and 'Roller Coaster'); and
Gloucestershire and Avon Life (for 'Cotswolds').

The man who takes our coins on the gravel track
is perched with a polythene box upon his knees;
another, strolling, hands behind his back,
keeps one eye on a comical Great Dane
that trots among the geometric trees

made for a stage set: all part of the plot
pretending this is just another scheme
to raise funds for the Red Cross, a spot
where ladies who like claiming, naming things
take tea and cuttings, strawberries and cream.

But what mind dreamed these twisting boulevards?
How can we prove the well-repeated tale
that a love-sot built this folly only yards
from his betrothed bed? For still the house keeps
a blind silence; there are no guides for sale.

From those windows, no union might be guessed:
all routes submerged in a junction-box of brick
where girls emerge from tunnels, looking perplexed,
and couples ask 'is this where we came in?',
unwitting victims of a twilight trick.

Is it a whale's rib, or distressed wood
that shocks us as we round a sudden bend?
The rest is a threadbare maze from childhood,
half recollected, a crazy pilgrimage
of which the outset is forgotten, the end

never quite believed in. Recurring figures snake
above our heads or beyond a gurgling stream
that slides from oblong holes to a distant lake
where fat goldfish, like scattered mosaics,
nose through lily-pads, in some other dream—

drowned souls perhaps, or ancient overlords
saved by knowing the right path from the wrong,
who stepped as we do now, over quaking boards
to a leaky boat and summer-house, where, lost
and loth to rebegin, we long to belong.

9

The white lamp coaxes shadows;
its glowing implies need;
as much a hint of failure
as a nurse is, weaving among beds
her smile of hope.

It hangs where flaring orange falters—
a private, not a municipal thing:
in alleys, or where handrailed steps
are swallowed by a shell-arched door.

It flickers on its bracket
as the carriage jolts away.
When wheels rumble over drain-hatches
and footsteps fade
it is a smudged gleam in wet slabs,
a pale hand edging a curtain
against the night.

The white lamp shifts
with a firefly sway
across a coastline
flecked with storm.
An earth-chained moon.

The white lamp has gone out,
its legend shrunk
to a tavern's name, creaking;
a dusty globe of fly-stuck glass,
forever cold.

THE ARCHAEOLOGIST

(for Bill Britnell)

Soil in his nails,
shirt, bones, dreams:
a worm grins and slides round sherds;
tight he curls in his tent below stars,
his thumbprint in the clay.

The earth holds runes he reads;
we see stones, and clumsily scuff
rare feathers, wherein
he traces empires.

On a government grant he indulges
obsession with phantoms;
tax on a navvy's sweat
supports his scratchings.

Where bulldozers charge and
excavators grapple,
he tracks
with his trowel and sharp eye,
like a seagull,

hoping to glean what the monsters neglect—
scraps of an older habit
when once we split the baked crust
that nursed no relics
but lay, cooling. . .

THE MIRROR

This mirror is not rigid on a wall;
though small, it won't sit in your hand,
        or slip into a bag.

Too liquid, this glass—

a pool you cup within two palms,
it weeps a pearl to parallel each drop
that seeps through leaking fingers.

In the vessel of your head
it slops around,
soaks the blotter of your brain,
snakes icy down your neck.

As you walk, you sense it
rocking, threatening to spill
—a thin-stemmed glass of sound.

Traffic vibrations,
jostle of crowds,
or sudden voice of a friend
can shatter it.

Picking through its sherds
for shapes you recognise,
your thumb is pricked to bleeding
on fragments of your face.

SMALL OBJECTS

('Small objects to represent our times are sometimes
placed in the foundations of a new public building
for future discovery. What items would you choose
for this purpose, and why?'
         Question on English Examination paper.)

Small objects
to represent our times
  —a pocket PacMan,
      Rubik's Cube, ignition key,
      Coke-can ring-pull, birth-pill foil,
      eraser tinted with strawberry essence,
      a blank-faced watch—

are sometimes placed in the foundations
of a new public building
  —dole centre, bingo hall,
      skating-rink, urinal,
      missile station, sauna bath,
      hypermarket, jail,
      burger bar, bierkeller, discotheque,
                                    boutique,
      sex-shop, sweet-shop, sweat-shop,
                              bus-stop,

—these few examples should suffice—

for future discovery
      by Martian? mutant? monk?
      or our children's children's children?
      gooseberry-hairy or fallout-bleached,
      clawing at the brickwork
      for memento
      or crust—

what items would you choose
for this purpose
and

Why?

SPACE BALL — MADE IN TAIWAN

(*a found poem*)

This item Space ball is knockdown style.
Please read before apply and partronize.
Inseart rotating part into U-shaped holder,
Check to prevent exceptionally tightness.

After assemble please put in plastic frame.
Push more powerfully at first time.
Must keep clean for U-shaped holder:
Add oil to increase rolling ability.

After revolving for period of time
Balls will not turn by qualitative principle:
Touch by hand is needed for balls to spin again.

All balls are composed of two parts.
If balls are separate, press one side on another
And the ball will be combined.

IMPLEMENT

Refiner of bluntness,
exposer of black hearts,
sharp practice is my game.

I perch on your desk's edge
in a guileless pose
that threatens revolution.

From off the slender legs of crayons
I peel fine hosiery,
and store within my gullet
a clutch of rainbow scrolls.

Into my orifice
your pencil fits snug:
like a lover I coax it
to a vibrant dart.

IN THE SEARCH ROOM AT ALEXANDRA HOUSE, KINGSWAY

They check my bag for bombs
in the library of death,
then I am free,
hang up my coat and scan the labels,
spread my notes across the table
where all the dead are roused,
and reach down a ledger
bulky with loss.

So many names with the same initial:
my own is one small pile of dust
in a one day pocket
a century ago.

Such a huddle of parishes:
from Tenterden, Newport Mon., St Pancras,
they were inked and shut away,
obsequious to time's regulation.

First I locate them,
then spare a fiver to plumb their starker facts,
queuing and form-filling over again
as they once did
who trudged to make the doleful news official
from undertaker to probate, to registrar,
through cold streets that caught their breath,
rehearsing time and again
the statistics of bereavement.

Twilight at four:
the room empties.
They stand again with no gaps in their ranks,
uniformed in bruise-and-midnight blue,
supporting each other, having shaken off
another day's assault,
their rest disturbed for grim speculation;
their worn paths
are ink-traces now,
quaintly curling on steel shelves,

while luminous, beyond locked doors
the streets of London
brace themselves for night.

TO A FOREBEAR

Two months ago, I'd never heard your name;
    family elders, kept in the dark,
    knew only that you drank. For a while
I coveted the fortune you could have swilled away.

Now I've no illusions, I try to imagine
    how the rumours grew. Three brothers;
    two were left, and you, hanging around,
stacking their timber, picking up the crumbs.

Somewhere a logical link. Your son,
    my misty grandad, kept his silent
    dignity, in the manner of those times.
Such wariness breeds fantasies.

I try to piece the past together
    but so many bits are lost
    that no-one but the dead I pick among
in trying to set it straight

Can complete the picture now.
    I am left to conjecture
    where you went, and when, to mull over
returns of census, graveyard records, wills.

Even your christening was an afterthought.
    By fourteen you had flown,
    leaving no trace, from the green hamlet
where your forebears had worked stone.

I sensed a skeleton, a door
    shut on the past. And I am the first
    resourceful and removed enough
to dredge you from the murk of time's canal.

There, in black and white, grossly public,
    an inquest, nineteen hundred and five.
    Your widow, Sophie, loaded with it all,
was 'put away' within living memory.

You were the withered branch.
   From it I too hang.
   Stained-glass windows to your uncle's glory
shed little light on us.

In a backstreet near his factory
   you shadowed his name, shouldered his deal.
   What could he have said to his Band of Hope
when you smashed the crockery?

To name you now in verse, Charles Henry,
   exhumes you from a vanished grave.
   Lie easy. Time has soothed away
the rages, the sorrow, the inequitable fame.

HOOVER

Call me a sucker? By making a nothing
I take all in; a mechanical snout
that gropes under skirtings for secreted filth,
renders to the widow her Lost Coin
with a rattle.

Aye, whiner and windbag. But don't be without me
before Christmas, cocktails, or such celebrations.
My belly is a bag of spent days
bound for the trashcan.
I scour the path of soles.

Dust have you sown, so you shall reap.
At your spickest hours I confront you
with this, your inheritance,
that speckles you constantly
but unheeded.

THE DISCOVERY

Something that I never missed,
lodged in the grass for a generation,
grows solid now, emerges in sharp light:
I see it for the first time.

There is only me to claim it.
It rears up to greet me
as if we're drawn together
over oceans and days.

I never thought to seek it, need it—
kept trim all these years
by keepers of a garden
I have never met,

all unaware of me
for monumental reasons;
a secret, buried so deep it became
a wordless conspiracy.

Its roots were in fear,
a shadow on the heart,
thought of as a stain,
a spot of blood,

most of all, blood lost,
and, like all loss, a seed:
a death, a sacrifice,
decidedly a love.

I leave it where it stands
rooted in itself,
touch it finally,
thank it for life,

and walk off
wrapped in a peace,
feeling myself whole
for the first time.

DOUBLE-SIDED COIN

(*for Alan Brownjohn*)

On Friday nights, when the round was extra-long,
I'd grub through the heavy bag of change
for bun-pennies: thin flat Pontefract cakes
worn smooth by a century's hands.

This one was nondescript to look at:
a stolid copper, Britannia boldly embossed,
with her Raleigh bike-wheel, gripping her trident.
Yet tubby round the middle.

A freak. A Siamese twin of coinage,
headless too. Its plaited tails
could not agree which birth to certify:
1926 or 1932?

I think now that someone's handy dad
had wrought this dud in a workshop,
but the trainspotter in me could only imagine
thundering drivers, coins quivering on the rail.

Wherever its forge, it had found a home.
If pennies ran out, this talisman
was never spent, but remained
deep in its seam with fluff and hardened gum.

Except when taken out for use.
As I flicked its double weight
to twirl against the sun, I'd stand
secretly gleeful, smug of all outcomes.

In matters deemed worth a toss, it was
my philosopher's stone, turned
any wind my licked finger burned with
to a captain's choice:

on a drying pitch, we deployed our spinners;
in a baking noon we batted first;
any advantage life afforded
my headless serpent helped me seize.

This at least was the dream.
But I lacked the killer-instinct,
afraid perhaps of some wrathful God
whose triple heads would one day repay.

Jurisprudence somewhere in my blood
made me smile and spin again
with legal tender. The freak that Fate
had foundered in my change was put away.

I could have been a millionaire,
cheating my way to a fortune (for some
the only way), always keeping
one hand in my pocket, never allowing

the secret of success to be revealed.
It never is. I keep it in a tin
at the top of the house, hidden somewhere
so lost I doubt if I could find it.

Now it's no use to my children. Times and coins
have changed. I wonder if they'll understand
the choice I made. If not, I know
I've no-one but myself to blame.

Tired, how vulnerable he is—my son,
crushed utterly by a last straw, and another,
and another.
              Hurling the dice to the floor
he sweeps aside
the rules we all conspire against him.
His mind is a snakepit, brimming.
All rungs greased to spite him. And
the real stairs now: the inevitable evasion
he knew would come. And howls
at their very mention.
                  All the long way
up.
   Why, after his dogged mast-
ery,
   keeping
firmly
     to the squares,
should odds be set against him?
Why
    is life
        such a climb?
Why
    must clothes be folded,
face swabbed, teeth scoured,
the bed always be cold?

              I leave him
with a random kiss,
ready for the darkness,
and trudge downstairs to scattered counters,
bits of food,
dishes and papers piled,
a dying fire.

Tired, how vulnerable we are, my son.
And the blows keep coming, keep coming,
keep coming.

Once, between my knees, I pumped him,
a liquid eel, into the hot dark of birth.

Now, his own knees
pin my elbows to the floor,
eager for revenge for all those soggy months
he sprawled growing.

His limbs, no longer matchwood,
are taut coils
to keep me in my place,
wedged between a chairleg and the door,
my very lankness a factor he exploits
as he twists in a space
smaller but freer than a womb.

Exertion once was sufficient to fling him,
a grain of grapeshot lost against the sky
from a knee-jerk:

now he rides my fiercest buckarooing,
teeth locked in a decisive snarl.

Being donkey, I cannot throw him off
except with a spasm so horrendous
it would snap his back and all the rules.

He doesn't gasp and flop back fish-like
as he used to when I kept it up for long,
but grinning, sits it out, learning to pace
his lungs, heart, and eye for time.

It is me who throws in the sponge,
invents a bedtime, or some burning need
to clang the bell for the final round,

he who comes back, a day later, wanting more,
sensing the long drawn out victory
cannot be put off.

He is here for good.

SCARECROW

Old rags for what? At first perplexed,
but remembering it's her day at playgroup
I cotton on: the seeding season,
'First the farmer sows. . .' —they're making a scarecrow.

Turning out pockets, I find a programme.
Four years ago this jacket mattered,
as it swished from bar to auditorium.
Now its lining hangs in tatters.

Gaudy socks, torn-crotch trousers, are stuffed
into the bag. And from the dressing-up bin
is trailed, like a conjuror's ribbons,
a college scarf, its colours now worn thin.

We dump the kit at the frowsty hall,
garden canes, old *Gazettes*, a ball of string.
Here amid glee, they create him, 'Worzel',
and prop him where he startles me coming in.

Soon I cannot face him. Switching on the light
as I go for a book or call of nature,
I panic at my own substantial shadow,
ill-at-ease with this twin silent watcher

He has to go, for the purpose intended.
At dusk I bear his cross, spike it in soil.
Through the night he stands, decked with my follies,
dewed with glinting medals, moonlight his foil.

PLAYGROUND

The child climbs, vulnerable on iron,
treads the steps of air, proving his growth,
and feels the sky build around him,
as people shrink below.

No gateman where the cage
frames dark stripes on the blue.
Gold river swoops to the stones.
Blood surges. Wind in his tears.

Known legs straddle the unfenced end,
a smile learnt by heart,
and hands that lift him, baby again,
in his levelling flight.

Firm earth he cannot bear:
impelled to move, he fountains back,
ascends the glinting iron alley
that brightens as it thins.

There the cage; still no-one;
a turnstile of wind clicks in his hair;
hills whirl, unseen before,
clouds tumbling, birds' mocking cries.

Below him, no shute
polished by rain and generations;
only the glitter of light, dark tree-groves,
a far-off twisting lane.

He'd call for them to mend it,
if they could be seen,
but no figure is there to bridge
the void he must leap

alone, buoyed by his own heartbeat,
sensing the turnstile rigid behind him,
and up the steps of pitted shadow
strange shoes clang.

Wharton Park, Durham

The kids squeal every time.
A fair parked in a lay-by
means a fair in the offing,
no matter how far from home.

We try to impress them
with a road's realities,
but speckled by exhaust-dust,
the images leak through:

tarpaulined shapes and painted cars,
colours unlike anything on the road,
and the lorries themselves:
bullet-headed Scammels, tyres like biceps,
tattooed heroes at the wheel.

Before we are round the bend,
they have pieced a hasty jigsaw,
from the chains and burnished fenders,
have built themselves a playpark in the mind.

A ferris wheel
spins its ball of sunlight;
a surging organ wheezes;
a waltzer flings their breath.

We tell them that it's all another season,
that they're homing for the winter
to oily ramshackle sheds,
to spend their rolling pennies
on sardines and beer,

but we can't get through:

soon we too are lost
in candyfloss meadows
where calliopes hoot and siren,
and gilded roosters twirl,

despite the unwinding road,
the dust and roaring,
tyres blundering over cat's eyes,
the lay-by's stock of grit.

ROLLER COASTER

It's a long way down
but over quick;
the kite of a scream
is winched back in,
as serpent cables tighten
the rack they undergo.
Cars grind up
a corkscrew track
to a deeper
stomach-churning drop.

And who they are up there
we never know;
to hear their torn recanting
is enough;
they have chosen,
paid and chosen, and now
they pay again,
exposed to our stares.
For who can pass and not
look up, to see them
balanced, ready to drop
with a squeal that pinches nerves?

Clattering trucks disgorge
a tottering cargo,
swallow more:
huddling girls who blush through candyfloss,
swaggering boys, urgent for ordeals.

It's a long, long way up.

Their world tilts, like a painting,
shakes and screams;
while we stand watching,
impotent, remote,
with one foot in their dreams.

MEMORY

A solid enough ghost,
too dead to haunt me now
on that narrow path he sentried,

but the young need teaching 'Fear'
and I resurrect him,
recall for every Third Year class
the twilight-silvered railings,
where I hauled my clattering bike
and swung to face him.

It's then the fear burns.
They grow quiet as I tell it
as if they feel it too:

night wind in my scalp,
feet forcing down the pedals,
wheels squealing into unknown cul-de-sacs.

I describe to them the face:
a furtive mask of shadows, crawling with . . .
What?

It's as much that grimy bandage, hanging loose,
as what it might hide,
as much the nearby angels, frozen in marble,
as what he might DO,

his fixing on this alley between graves.

Did he recognise my panic
when, my lamps unlit,
I turned and fled?

Was this what he intended?
knowing, in a life
gnawed by regret,
his one remaining duty:

to instruct the young in 'Fear'?

THE HEAD

Above all else—a mouth;
source of no word, no sound;
betraying no emotion
—no cry, nor mirth, nor shock;
an inexpressive gape
straight from a dentist's chair.

But no bone neither:
no grinding molars there,
no hinge for a hovering snap.

Receptacle solely.
A passive mouth,
yawning for whatever
we care to drop in.

Coloured bulbs play tag
above this lurid trophy,
infusing him with moments
of jaundice, rage, envy,
then the ice-bruise of blue.

The head moves too:
back and forth it glides
in a slow insistent 'n o'.

These are the jaws of chance:
passionless features too bland
for subterfuge.
I swop my coin for three small plastic globes,
weightless as reasons,
blown tight as hope,

and drop them
one by one
down his gulping throat,
watch them
teetering then scuttled
through angled slats of wood.

The arithmetic is wrong.
Three ping-pongs huddle sheeplike
in their pre-ordained rows.
A stranger is pocketing my coin.
Like the head itself,
dowsing with its heart
the tilted board,
he doesn't bat an eyelid,

but goes on bawling to the crowds, agog,
'roll up, roll up.'

TRESPASS

A doorway into shadows.

Inside, a barn
of shifting sulphur air.
Ash pits.
Purgatorial fumes.

Long slow breaths—
ours, or the sleepers'?

Engines, like leviathans,
lying, nose to tail;
inert iron girdles.
Our eyes, adjusting to the darkness,
are level with their flanks
as we stalk between.

Echoing clang
like armour dropped
or weapon forced from hand
in the daybreak world
where light leaks in.

A snort,
billowing steam,
makes our ears sing,
the ground shudder:

something has risen to its feet,
and lumbers away.
Light slides across its steel.

The hulks around us,
sunk in gloom,
are motionless and cold.

Soot tickles in my throat.
A cough
startles the reeking air,
sends shock-waves shunting.

It cannot wake
the things we stalk in awe of,
their domes high in darkness,
muffled by cowls;

but it may rouse one
figure of our fears:
the dapper man
in overalls and bowler
who barks official warning,
whose thumb and finger
tweezers our ears.

Forgotten
and only now remembered:
November's damp sacking,
cold flannel slapping the face,
ruined warehouse skies.

Summer's oozing brass shrunk
to a thin silver wailing,
as the Armistice circus,
poppied and buttoned,
hugs its euphonium grief
and stamps
one final beat of dignity
on the sluggish wind-shone road.

COBBLER'S SHOP, GLOUCESTER FOLK MUSEUM

And so I am drawn to the cobbler's shop,

to its leather smell, its scattered scraps,
ugly tools like crippled hands,
their blackness worn to glints
in the pauper light.

I know what haunts me here:
dead feet stood to attention on the shelf,
toeless and unlaced.

Too much here of the low corner-hut,
always gloomed, but oddly silent now
in the fly-buzzing swelter, wreathed by the stink
of horse-dung from the road.

And the glossier parlour opposite,
its curtains drawn on an unheard knocking,
joints more durable,

where the cobbler lies, in odorous shade,
his heels grown dark,
like these relics of his trade
in the shuttered sun.

AN OLD FRIEND

(for George Conway)

Your number's in the book,
buried in a pile
like an attic souvenir:
plumbers long since out of business,
dead uncles, emigrated friends,
weave cobwebs round your name.

When I dial,
baffled how to greet you,
no smug purr delivers
the password to your den,
but a high-pitched whine.

Enquiries cannot help:
official records blank you out.
Yours is a discontinued line;
your initials a lost cause.
Our thread sheared through.

The Library's shelf of Directories
rises like a cliff.
Cardiff ? London? Bournemouth—
where we last met, one afternoon,
on roads that led elsewhere?

And why this urge to meet you?

After ten years of paying you no heed,
something rises in me
like a creature from a lake;
and bubbles surface with it—
images we share:

> the model locomotive
> stretched cat-like on your windowsill
> outfaces its ancestral hulks
> in the soot-caked engine shed;

your aunt, who forks the steaming pan,
her hair a wisping coil
of fuse-wire, shrieks you out
to the corner-store,
and demands exact change;

later, in adjacent beds,
your Law textbooks between us
as we talked, late into the night,
of the Welsh-cake girls we'd nuzzled
beneath suburban lamps.

Are you trying to get through?
—dialling my old number from some New Town box,
rattling the cradle, and hearing,
as I did,
that lonely existential sound:

the wind in the wires,
'number unobtainable',
subscriber gone to ground.

He waves at all the cars.
Uncertain whether he knows us or is crazy,
most of us wave back.
It gets to be a habit.

For months I never saw him,
never missed him,
for you don't miss a wave
when your foot is down.

Perhaps, wherever he had been,
he took time to adjust,
to recognise the regulars,
but his gesture came once more—

a stick this time, shaken
with a grim determination
against whatever had laid him low
—damned if he couldn't wave.

From childhood mists, his counterparts
come swimming. Like ruddy Jack,
bulldog-jawed, potato-sack man
who hailed in the same brash way.

Streets full of veterans;
one-legged newsvendor, hawking
headlines from the kerb;
bandaged phantom at graveyard gates;

another who cursed his fat mongrel
then tommy-gunned the buses;
he calls them all back
with his grim wave.

Always car-bound, unable to stop,
when I've seen him,
as if in rushing by
we taunt him with what passes:

as they all will soon,
these men who stalk the streets on sticks,
wearing their wounds and memories
under their coats, like medals.

OBSERVATORS

(for Terry Sharpe)

Masons of a mystery;
their rare smiles,
eyes fixed ahead,
and gold-braided cloaks
all said so.

Men towering over boys—
one had a moustache.
A different breed:
even on bikes
they preserved their dignity.

A Corps Elite,
never capricious.
They ruled
without rods
our patched backstreet ways.

Sons of men
who rose on platforms,
wore suits,
drove cars,
were models beyond.

Years later, blazoned,
setting my examples,
seeing through their eyes,
I could not don
their flapping gowns—

no more than
I could fly.
Shrouds,
billowing phantoms
of all I should avoid.

SEYMOUR ROAD

(for 'Chet' Sly, wherever he is)

Hooters at noon,
white plume above the timber-yards;

adverts for pies and turf accountants
slide along the glass above the door;

rumble of trainwheels, streets away,
where a cycle phalanx storms the red-shield gates.

Hooves stamp in the corporation depot;
whisper of hay through iron airvents;

Thundering steamroller flywheel,
marble clattering over leaf-clogged drains.

Whiff of yeast from the thistled bakehouse;
at the cobbler's door, a rubber-heel of dark.

Chimneys felled;
sleepers, fish-plates, drawn like teeth;

Flickering scythe of pigeons
harvesting the sun.

Above the rows of lofts and rhubarb
your window winks at the night.

FOR KEITH T.

A long term for you,
though being absent you missed
the endless yellow sheets,
frayed nerves,
the sullen chafing leavers.

Spring broke at last,
bursting through the hill like water
to silver your face
as you walked thin-scalped,
surprising those who met you.

How well you had done!
As if the whole affair were the long stretch
at Claypits with the wind in your teeth,
a set of weights,
a tough class.

Today, hooking up my helmet
I saw your spare clothes on a peg
and waited for your banter
as ruddy and laughing
you'd steam in from the road.

In a snatched lunch, on Maiden Hill,
I recall the one we shared at Frampton,
a bonus in the snow;
how its mention would set a log-fire
blazing within you.

I kick at grass
of the rough pasture
and think how you must miss
this season's scruffy heads,
these dandelions,

each year's beacons,
though common as the clods
that they are turning,
even now,
over you.

44

TURNSTILE MAN

Ticket vandal;
counts his victims in a squealing cog;
architect in coinage:
bruises the monarch with a spring-snap,
soon satisfied.

Lawless crowds that block traffic
flock to his temple,
his twilit arch:
flesh pinioned—
mute gestures of hands.

From screwed gloves and chewed nails,
work-scarred palms,
smouldering butt and
rolled papers,
his eyes fork silver.

One eye mirrors flags
on Elysian greens;
the other— bodies
shuttering the light,
edging, tight and expectant.

He's Peter, keyless,
or in this gloom, Charon,
conscious of no office but
production-line motion,
the rare flung 'thankyou'.

CARETAKER

(*for Andrew Wood*)

No-one does the things taken for granted
if I don't:
sweep the stairs,
set the chairs in a circle,
hook crushed worms from rancid ashtrays.

Who else makes the glass gleam,
flushes milk from jugs,
smooths the mats where acrobats spring;
who can make the blue flame
leap in its grille?

They never notice
all their art depends on
until it's undone;
their undoing is what I mend
at the end of the day,

slide bolts on doors
they're not aware of,
projection-box, pantry,
glory-holes
where easels and cellos are bundled away.

No-one sees this place in a morning light,
its pyramids of dust,
folded packs of chairs.
No-one smells its pent-up damp,
Art's vacant chill.

Echoes of applause
sink in the tissue-bin
as I fade the lights,
leaving one bloodshot eye
guarding the dark.

WAITRESS

Where did she learn that look?
Her cockatoo head jerks,
beak squawks disjunctive noises,
blonde feathers toss.
Dark eyes punctuate her message,
wings folded onto hips,
her body balanced, perching.

Caged in this canteen
there's little space for preening.
Her clipped cries
chirp through steaming morsels,
crisp-bags, ash-flecked cups.

Wherever she was fledged
she's suited here,
has found a home for her style
among tiles and formica.

FIVE SWIMMERS

I

Straight in and down, down,
thinned to a blurr, a shark, a torpedo;
suddenly tight for air, he
thrashes into light, throwing off the pool
like a hot blanket; his surprise
at surfacing among kids
soon swept aside with his flapped hair
and he's off again, shoulders churning,
slicing a soon-flooded path to the other side.

II

Baptises her body a moment, to keep cool;
but never long out of her depth, glides back
to perch and be seen at her most revealing,
not too impressed by the slim young man who,
chest-hair flashing medallions on the high board,
plunges seal-like to her silent command.
Hugging her knees on bikini'd breasts,
she tosses her mane and blinks her desires
to the blue light-sparked lagoon.

III

Here on doctor's orders, dot of nine, however
cold the dawn or waters, taking the plunge
back to health, goaded by the spectre
of his own decline, leering through the glass,
or stiffly inert, a black crack, on the bed below.
Six, hard labour, on his back, slowly,
then, as the air fills with unpredictable boys,
a frog-like crawl. Is that his cap, that dome
that glides and bobs, or a wrinkling skull?

IV

Come not for herself, but in love and duty,
bearing a body that makes the children stare,
—the stretchmarked skin, her Leviathan hugeness—
mother and mother-to-be, a human lifebelt,
pilots the child in tow and the child inside her
kindly into shallows. Another child within,
a self long-submerged, is born anew
as her thighs are launched on remembered seas
and her smock swirls round her, like a hoop of flowers.

V

These are the ones we watch from the snackbar,
the true entertainers, the young. Snorting,
cavorting, even courting along the water-line;
look-at-me jackknives, badges on their trunks,
brown legs that hinge to the springboard rhythm,
hooking costumes over pert buttocks and leaping,
laughing droplets from their eyes. Their behaviour
is water-behaviour, full of surprises.
Smaller ones, goggled tadpoles, crawl from stones.

Spotlights, amber sunsets,
glint in rows of dimpled glasses,
turned-wood pillars,
stacked blue cartons
in the cigarette machine.

Smoke plaits from glass-tray bonfires
of solitary men unwinding
in the small hours after tea.

A pin-stripe suit leans an elbow
on a fruit machine.
The barman slices lemons,
fills a jug.

Something ought to be about to happen;
nothing is,
but the encroach of night,
the trickle of grey time.

From speakers out of sight behind the panelling,
a steel guitar begins to whine,

softly,
not to disturb these early drinkers,
who swill the bitter liquors like a mouthwash,
and finger their coins.

SHEDS

From the landing window
looking down at sliced gardens
I noticed the sheds
wedged at ends of concrete paths
like dumped luggage.

The nondescript houses
yoked with sculleries' roughcast
as if linking for a conga
seemed to have spawned these ridged shacks
in some mad fling.

The best reared acutely
over levelled slabs and swept benches,
housing the honed and gleaming tools
to which they owed their fashion,
proud of their pedigree.

Others wore peak caps,
stood stiffly, arms akimbo
to marauding winds and rain,
rusted padlocks like clenched fists
guarding bikes and mowers.

A few, tottering,
shabby with foot-rot and webbed eye,
held forgotten, loose-hinged foibles,
the flaking past, put by in hope
for makeshift futures.

ALLEYS

The best are bollarded and cobbled,
flanked by mossy walls
with glimpses into lawyers' book-lined rooms
or knot-holes in fencing
framing white chairs on a lawn.

Tin plates forbidding cycles
can't extinguish secret dreams
of gaslit doors where mobsters rendezvous.

On dreary days
they threaten new perspectives,
turn contracts lost
into hairbreadth triumphs
by their sneakered sprints round cut corners.

Puddled ruts by garage-blocks
past someone's kidney beans;
scoops of shade through pink-wash bungalows;
decayed backstreets, dotted on maps,
that loop, thread, but never quite meet
as they leapfrog the town;
or dripping diversions
of not much in particular
round hospital fire-escapes,
chain-store loading-bays:

they are at least alternatives;
for the hasty often the best way out,
and for the lucky, the lost, the flashy,
they are havens,
unlatched windows,
slipways in.

HANG GLIDER

Hawk, a fragile tremble,
tricks our sight above shifting trees
where hillside sinks to a tussock tide,
snares us, breeding an awe
akin to the weasel's panic
caught at woodland edge.

But a new shadow
sweeps our upturned gazing:
a cumbersome bird, that swoops, tilts,
jousting with the wind,
a bone-frame to fracture or be flung;
man become hawk, scouting for sensation.

Gymnast of gilt and mottled lights
he feints designs on the unmapped air
in a tantalising puppetry.
Intent on our sky-thrown prophet,
absorbed in his ascending,
we are envious, perhaps, or remember Icarus.

No novelty that holds us (though we marvel less
at airborne hulks of steel, or the kestrel's
dappled beauty), but our own shape
turned to bird, dreams at last made flesh
and flashed across the hills: our dicing
solitary selves we grapple with up there.

INCIDENT AFTER A FESTIVAL

(for Mhairi)

Open-flapped tents,
chords strummed in lit cornfields,
leaning emerald hills,

and a grey woman
among yellowed stalks of bruised grass
squeezed a plaintive concertina.

Back at the house,
a door-jamb of mail
toys upturned,
cups festering on ledges.

On a blanket in the kitchen
where our neighbour had spread him
lay a mat of tabby
patched with blood.

Through snatched jigs of a fiddle
I remembered the phone-call.

Buffed by a hurtling shadow
he had spilt into the kerb
like a jigsaw,
one eye bulging
in the light of moons
that had pierced him,
reeling.

Now his old fur
rose and fell,
oozing one sour note
like a duff bagpipe.

*

On the vet's table, we watched him
worked like a marionette,
shoulder sagging,
jelly sickly red.

A needle pierced his neck
and he flopped, relieved,
on the stained formica.
'Bring him tomorrow if he lives.'

We hoped he'd not:
bruised grass, snared with
strains of a festival.

AFTER THE WOODPECKER

(for Mike Mockler)

Mosquitoes dart and nip
Everywhere; rhododendrons
Suck and smother the soil;
    the earth is hard,
    the eyehole small,
But the woodpecker can make up for everything.

She knew we were there:
Shirt bright in sunlight
Made her cock her head,
    rattle her grub-filled
    throat, and wait,
Leaning back from her trunk like an abseiler.

The classic pose, beak
Poised, not to peck
But to plunge, to where
    her young clustered,
    hungry and clicking
Like clocks just assembled and not quite the ticket.

I shall let them all know,
In wash-basin banter,
Through dinner-plate clatter,
    or briskly down corridors
    past close-shut rooms:
The woodpecker can make up for everything.

BULLOCKS

Rooted in their mud-yard
their frayed bell-pulls twitch
in a wind too cold for flies.

Foreheads curly-permed,
flanks a mountainside of burnt bracken,
black rings round their eyes.
Their horns are toddlers' handlebars.

Pink strap tongues like sucked nougat
flick from heels of snakeskin shoes
to trap spaghetti shreds of hay;
cheeks pump like fish-gills as they chew.

One stares me out,
as he impudently jets
a stair-rod of pee
to fix him where he stands.

These are their winter quarters,
a dusk-filled country chapel
that reeks like a teapot,
an ankle-deep soup of their own churning.

Patience itself,
they digest growth and slaughter,
shift their weight like sentries
with a wet slap,
and snort with the same flat slurp,
the only tune they know,
but for the wind rasp in the thorn hedge,
the steel gate's shuddering clang.

CHESSBOARD WEATHER

It's chessboard weather,
and we, its pawns,
are sharp-toed, bake-headed,
as we crunch across a slice of shade
that cuts like trip-wire.

Upper air is desert air
pampering the face,
but under walls and ditches
frost lurks, like spies
holding out till nightfall.

Freighted with fur, we perspire,
seduced by spring,
only to pucker and set
in wind's chill corners.
No wonder we are schizoid,

temperate beings, lured
by snowlight's spicy glitter,
curfewed by twilight's ambush,
and by mid-morning's cross-fire
wounded in the thigh.

It's hot enough already:
my breakfast cup's the only thing awake;
the radio I silenced in its prime—
who wants hot news now?
Foment of statistics,
salacious expectations
when the sun's wide blade
flashing from the east
thickens the tension
before birds have stopped quarrelling
or traffic wardens come.

The journal thrusts a slot of toast
into the catacomb hall.
I pluck it, drop it unread,
sucking my fingers,
go to shower instead.

On the stairs, the drapery of air
fondles my face like hired wenches.
I run the window's gauntlet,
feeling fired arrows burn.

Cubicled drops stipple the puckered skin
where damp sheets lately clung;
temperature predictions, crime figures,
by-election margins, go
swirling down the drain.

Outside, the park airs its blanket
for the noontime breadcrumb stripshow;

the drinking fountain polishes its shoes.

Today the world will buckle
ten degrees further.
Skirmishes are stirring in my blood;
in the head, muffled tomtoms,
opening salvoes.

We must have missed the crack. If there was one.
But who would risk the thumbscrews and the rack
For a quick squeeze of synthetic cream?
Someone fired by the hot cross on the buns?
An Easter miracle? Did three hours' darkness
Rend this temple's veil, in a divine passion
For doughnuts? Or a near miss for the church
Five doors away?

                At first we feared a closure,
A worked-out seam in our Lardy Cake Mine,
Or a sticky-fingered young assistant
Absconding with the jam.

                Whatever our theology,
Walking early on Easter Day, we found
The shutters up, the town's sweetmeat display
Censored, like a sex-shop boarded blind.

Then this morning, men in overalls
Worked to release the first warm whiff of bread
And tore away the shopfront's mouldy crust.
While early housewives crinkled splits and baps
They knelt in sunlight, kneading putty-dough,
Spreading thick the wafers of wood and stone.

Their crowning glaze is barely visible—
Brought from the van and slotted into place,
A flawless slice of light.

                And now, outside,
Office-workers, children, pensioners with dogs
Cluster, pressing their noses to this glass,
Mesmerised by cherries, custard, jam,
Like winking jewels, that will not let them pass.

NIGHT WIND

Boot-studs on the felting
splinter our sleep.

Ears clenched with commotion,
nerves padlocked into fear,

the body's deadweight
hunched in a dream-fug.

Light shunts against walls—
the clang of wagons

and smokestack roar
as a coal-train thunders through

the tunnel of our head.
Hill rock stacked above.

COTSWOLDS

So much sky, and light, striking the stone
and green uplands. Crow and cloud-shadow
drift and wheel; sheep and farms in the folds.

Tumuli, spires, rutted tracks—relics
of older ways. Bones, fossils, quarries
breaching the skin. And the wind, always.

Nettles nod at stiles; orchids surprise
where cattle graze; and on darkening slopes
beeches stir and moan, splintering the sun.

A land for the solitary; pungent
in twilight; framed by mullion, lych-gate,
barn door; the silver river beyond.

THOUGHTS OF IVOR GURNEY, FROM GLOUCESTERSHIRE

Gurney missed all this: the life fulfilled,
Morning surge to work, the clattering chairs,
Earnest queues of public searching out
Your professional expertise.

The glass displays the Vale, gold and seeping
With last night's rain, spiked with winter trees
And sharp-edged buildings such as these,
Angled to catch this view:
Malverns, misted Wales, the glinting snake.

Out there lies Framilode, unspoiled still,
Threaded by ditches that trickle to the sea;
Washed white today like bleached bones
By the sprung nor'wester that twists grass,
Rasping sandflats where tide-harried logs
Crawl to convalesce.
                        His boat ages gone.

In a quagmire land of corpses, rats and fear
He no doubt saw this view: flashed by Verey lights
On a pane soon to crack. Beside him queued the public,
No longer quite so keen, khaki shadows, sick
Of professional expertise.

                        I missed all that:
Waste, carnage, madness—bitter wrack
Of lyric and content.

                        The sun strikes sharper,
Widens the hills in a perspective of peace.
I put away a folder as the room empties.
Shelling questions die away.
                        Now I can write.

CHICKEN MOON

In noon heat
our wrinkled Chinese neighbour
has chopped and chopped
at matted flax of turf
and cables of nettles;

his cheekbones glisten sweat
but his tireless arms
ginger up our shared neglected land
as his Dutch hoe
pecks at the clods
like a famished bird.

Now after nightfall
I fork his harvest
into the flames,
dodging the dragon's lunge
as it twists on a tail
tethered in orange heat.

The cabbages,
ragged silver sentinels,
huddle in their frost pools
and sport strange emblems
in homage to the moon.

How calm and luminous the night
as it drinks the smoke
from crackling twigs and pods.

A swollen boat
glides between cloud headlands
where surf piles silently
against a shore.

Stiff
in a basket under the hedge
is the crown of all this
consummation.
My fingers flick her waxy feathers
and squeeze her limbs
already setting
into the concrete of death,

before I place her
like a bundle of old secrets
or a final stone
where the bright tongues swell.

In this shadow theatre
of moon smoke and flame
her plumage turns to nettles,
her legs lilac twigs
until she's lost to sight.

Only when a richer
choking smoke
rolls across the air
like roasting beans,
trailing its veil across
the moon's made-up face,
do I retreat indoors,
throwing meaningless straws
in a final gesture
towards the hunched figure of heat.

Into my dreams I carry
the stab of prongs
that pierced her oozing bones,
the hot tang of her juices
on the blue felt of night.

In a mist-morning
by the ash-flecked privet,
I release her three sisters
to gobble the corn.

The Chinaman, up early,
on his haunches by the pyre,
now a whiskering heap of white,
tosses stalks
like the I-Ching
and chuckles toothily
'Good, very good'
(the only words we share),
as his shovel sifts the crystals
of my full-moon conflagration.

TIME AND WORDS

time and words
are not enough
to hoard the sensations
the old stirrings
that flit with a one-note song
and fly
from the foliage of the heart

sticks hewn from hedges
that grip the hand
like dying friends
and draw us out
over paths that startle and twist
through coppice and corn

a woman's hand
thrust in her hair
sculpture of ivory
and skeined silver
the mystery of her own making
through which she sings

clouds that roll and coalesce
slipping off their makeup
and tipping down
through dark-groined hills
leaving us only shadows
that rustle and turn pellucid
as the wind heeds our watching

time and words
can only whisper
sliding over stone
perpetual waterfalls
their use-worn corners
glossy in the light
of our suddden
soon-lost knowing

CALLIOPE

Calliope, she's chortling in the square,
an abacus of minims in the mote-freckled air,
while trolleybuses twirl, shoppers stop, stare
and dash for items they'd forgotten,
artichokes, elvers, blue-bag dye,
the little things, easily lost,
not from this year's list,
but scribbled long ago
in a child's doodling hand
on abandoned invitations.

Calliope cavorts
like waves along a promenade
of candystripe, whelks, and blue-jerseyed sailors;
giggles and hics and swells her song
with trawlermen in amber bars,
salt in her harmonies,
and melancholy green
beneath the foam.

Calliope she's brass,
wine-stout and scarlet
from too much song:
your deepest secret set to airs
and blared in carnivals,
lines too ripe to keep
from closing stanzas,
fluff-wrapped souvenirs you feared to find
on drowsy afternoons spent clearing drawers.

Calliope,
all she's got she'll share,
every siren, every snare
of her brassbound, loud,
and very pirate nerve.

Japamala ~~didi~~